SPEECHES
FOR ALL OCCASIONS

LINDA SONNTAG

MIMOSA
·BOOKS·

NEW YORK · AVENEL, NEW JERSEY

This 1993 edition published by Mimosa Books, distributed
by Outlet Book Company, Inc., a Random House company,
40 Engelhard Avenue, Avenel, New Jersey 07001

First published in 1991 by Grisewood & Dempsey Ltd.
Copyright © Grisewood & Dempsey Ltd. 1991

10 9 8 7 6 5 4 3 2 1

ISBN 1 85698 510 5

Printed and bound in Italy

CONTENTS

INTRODUCTION

It is a great honor to be asked to speak at a dinner, and yet many people would run a mile rather than stand up and talk to a roomful of friendly people. There is a general feeling that good speakers are born and not made, and a general suspicion that when the talent was handed out, it was handed out to other people.

This is fundamentally untrue. Everyone can learn the art of good communication, and everyone can learn to overcome the nerves that beset all speakers, even the professionals.

This book tells you about the kinds of speeches you might be called on to make and gives clear advice on how to prepare, rehearse, and deliver them. It explores the power of humor, helps you deal confidently and persuasively with your audience, and provides the background information you need to make sure that the event ahead runs smoothly. At the back of the book you will find a selection of classic speeches and quotations that you can draw upon in building up your own speech.

The skills necessary for public speaking are confidence of manner and clarity of thought and expression, allied to a belief in the worth of your message. These are the skills needed in job interviews and in social and business dealings, and to develop them will improve the way you communicate, not only with an audience, but also with friends and colleagues.

Freedom of speech is one of the basic human rights, and exercising it to the best of your ability is an exhilarating experience. This book aims to help you enjoy that experience to the full.

1 THE FORM

When you are asked to make a speech, the first essential is to find out what type of speech is required. It may be a toast, to an individual, or to a number of individuals, or to an organization. You could be called upon to respond to a toast, made to yourself or to the organization which you represent. You could also be asked to introduce a guest speaker, or to propose a vote of thanks.

The guest speaker is often a professional hired for the occasion, but if you, as an amateur, are undertaking this role, your job will be to get the message of the event across to your audience.

Never lose sight of the purpose of your speech while you are planning it, and remember to repeat it in simple words at the end of your address; it has been known for proposers of toasts to sit down without proposing a toast.

Proposing a toast

What exactly is a toast? The dictionary says it is a "tribute or proposal of health, success, etc., marked by raising glasses and drinking together." This convivial custom has its roots in medieval France, when a goblet of wine into which a piece of spiced toast had been dropped was passed between the guests, each one of whom raised the glass to the principal female guest, spoke her name, and took a draught of the drink. The last person to whom the goblet was passed was the lady herself. She would pick the wine-soaked toast from the glass and eat it. The charming idea behind this ritual was that the name of the lady would flavor the drink just as the spiced toast had done.

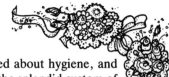

Today we are more enlightened about hygiene, and everyone has his own glass. But the splendid custom of drinking to a person's health and success remains, and the speaking of their name is preceded by a speech which takes its name from the piece of toast that used to spice the drinks all those centuries ago.

Toast to a host organization
Your hosts may be a company or corporation, a charitable society, a club, or they may be friends and acquaintances. Whoever they are, you must remember that you are paying tribute to them as a group. Although you may single out one or two people for special attention, in particular the chairperson, and perhaps also the person who is going to respond to your proposal, you should not add these names onto your toast, but finish simply by saying: "Ladies and gentlemen, let us raise our glasses to the Bloomfield Cycling Club," or whatever it might be.

Remember that you have been invited to celebrate the organization, and not to criticize it for its policy. Don't remind its members that the annual river trip had to be cancelled for lack of support or that the treasurer was fired for mismanaging the funds. Never dwell on regrets or mistakes. You are expected to say complimentary things, to mention goals achieved, sums of money raised, events well attended, accolades received, and/or prizes won.

Your speech will go down better if you have researched the organization's activities and successes over the past year. If it is a firm of California wine producers, you could say, for example, that the vineyards have expanded, the firm is now exporting its wine to France, and has just won an award from a leading wine magazine. You can mention the chairman, but without sounding too sycophantic.

If you yourself represent a sister organization, it may be appropriate to outline the similarities and differences between your two groups, and the suitability of any joint venture.

To make your speech more lively, you could include humorous references to one or two of the lighter-hearted events of the year. Indeed it is preferable to dwell for a moment on a few of the highlights than to give equal weight to a long list of items. One of the most boring things you can do is to give a blow-by-blow account of the minutiae of the year's business. No one will thank you, and some of the guests may well nod off before the toast is proposed.

A toast to the guests

It is customary for a member of the host organization to propose a toast to welcome the invited company. This is not a long speech, and should be thought of more in terms of introducing the most important guests. If you have been asked to propose this toast, find out the names and details of the principal official guests, who should be singled out for special mention, and also of any distinguished guests who may have been invited in a private capacity and who should also be presented to the company.

Remember that when you are introducing the official guests you should not concentrate on their personal qualities, but on the capacity in which they have been invited to attend. Unless you know the guests well, it is better not to refer humorously to them, but to keep your introductions short and succinct. Never say anything that could embarrass or offend.

In deciding which guests to mention by name, exercise the utmost tact. Make sure you don't hurt anyone's feelings by leaving them out, but on the other hand, remember that your audience doesn't want to listen to a list as long as Who's Who. Don't forget the ordinary members of your audience either – extend a generous welcome to all present, and end by proposing your toast: "Mr. Chairman, Mrs. Snowhaven, Mr. Porter, and honored guests!"

A toast to the chairman

If this toast falls to you, your job will be to highlight the attributes of the chairman that make him or her so good at the job. You will need to know something about his or her previous history before joining the present organization, as well as his or her achievements over the past year. Personal qualities of the chairman that benefit the club or company could happily be illustrated with reference to specific events.

Anecdotes will enliven your speech, but beware of over-familiarity. On the other hand, don't be too fulsome in your praise or too obvious in your flattery. Probably the best policy is to be selective with the truth, reflecting honestly the chairman's better points and leaving any dubious areas of character or management well alone.

A civic toast

This is similar to the toast to the chairman, but it is addressed to the mayor or other civic leaders who may be present. Again, attention should be focused on the person's achievements in their official capacity and kept off their private life. If you are proposing this toast you will need to research the activities of the civic community so that you can outline its history as well as give details of current events.

The special point to be made here is that you should avoid the temptation to give a political slant to your speech, remembering that the achievements of the mayor and town council are supposed to be beyond politics and for the benefit of the community as a whole. The mayor is the chief representative of the community, and in toasting him, you are toasting all its members.

A welcome to the ladies (or gentlemen)

This is a vague and, many feel, somewhat outdated piece of gallantry – a welcome to the opposite sex. If you have been asked to make this speech, you will no doubt be racking your brains for something original to say.

Try to avoid clichés, coyness, and flattery. If you keep your compliments to practicalities, thanking the partners of members of an all-women's or all-men's club for their support, for instance, you should be able to avoid sexism as well. Let the tone of your speech be friendly rather than insincerely flirtatious.

Its very vagueness makes this speech one of the most difficult to give, and your best bet is to stick to specifics and keep it short.

TIPS FOR TOAST-MAKING

* Stick to your brief and end your speech by making the toast required.

* Ask the gathering to join with you in drinking the toast, but avoid old-fashioned cliches like "please be upstanding."

* A toast should always be complimentary, never critical or contentious.

* Sincere praise is acceptable; sycophancy is not.

* Make sure you include any relevant names and achievements in your speech, but don't make it into a list.

* Research the background of the individual or organization you are toasting and use your information selectively.

* Enliven your speech with appropriate anecdotes.

Responses

Each toast will be followed by a response. In many ways, the person who responds to a toast has an easier job than the person who proposes it. Your basic duty is to thank the proposer for kind remarks. Next, you should comment on what you have just heard. Then you can give the audience some background information to explain why the proposer was so well placed to propose the toast in the first place. And finally, if it is appropriate, you can tell them why you have been chosen to respond.

The skill in giving this kind of speech lies in your ability to give an interesting and useful off-the-cuff response to the proposal. You should be able to do this easily, as no one should know more about the position you hold or the company you represent than you do yourself. Take care, though, not to give too much extra information about your organization or group if there is a danger that this will be covered by a subsequent speaker or speakers.

Responding on behalf of an organization

Your prepared remarks might center around plans your organization has for the future, which the proposer will not know about. But first you should thank him or her and elaborate on what has just been said, if appropriate.

The key to a successful response is to remain flexible, because after all, the first part of your speech has to be impromptu. Whatever you do, don't bore the audience with an interminable catalog of your organization's achievements, because there are few things more exhausting than listening to a list and, as the saying goes, self-praise is no recommendation. If you are going to praise anyone, praise the proposer.

Responding on behalf of the guests

The person who welcomed the guests will have been the host or a member of the host organization, and obviously someone well known, by reputation at least, to all present. So no explanations are necessary on that score. This speech is quite a simple one and can often be light-hearted in tone. All that is needed is an expression of thanks for the kind remarks of the host, and for the excellent evening being enjoyed by all.

The chairman's response

The chairman's speech can be the most important of the evening; it will certainly be a key speech in that person's career as chairman, and in the organization's year.

The chairman begins with an enormous advantage, which is that as leader of the organization gathered at the meeting he or she can be assured of the support of the whole audience even before beginning to speak. In a convivial atmosphere, past disagreements will be forgotten, momentarily at least, and unity will usually preside.

The chairman should begin with thanks to the proposer. Don't get carried away by the kind things he or she has said about you, and bear in mind that though the toast seemed personal, it came to you because you hold a particular office. Reply in kind, paying tribute where tribute is due. A courtesy you should not omit is to thank the organizers of the dinner. You should also be generous in praising fellow members of the organization you chair as you recount the achievements of the past year and talk of plans and hopes for the future. This is an opportune moment to outline to everyone the direction in which you hope your organization will go over the next twelve months.

Introductions

If there is to be a guest speaker, a member of the host organization will usually be asked to introduce him or her to the assembled company. If this job falls to you,

TIPS FOR RESPONDING TO A TOAST

* Don't get carried away by praise. Be concise and avoid elaborating on your own triumphs.

* Be scrupulous in thanking people: the proposer, organizers, and people who have helped and supported you.

* If appropriate, give a few biographical details of the proposer to put him or her in context for the audience.

* Be flexible. Be prepared to comment on the gist of the proposer's speech, but don't argue or criticize.

* Don't tread on the toes of the speakers who follow you by going beyond your brief.

* Remember that you usually begin with the audience firmly supporting you. Aim to keep their esteem, and don't weaken it by wearing them out with boring statistics.

you will need to find out all you can about the guest, including relevant details of past career, present occupation, and the reason that they were invited. The guest may have a special connection with your charity, for example, or may be coming to tell you about his or her travels in a part of the world that your club intends to visit.

Explain this briefly, without taking the words out of the guest speaker's mouth. You are not supposed to give a full speech yourself, but to whip up interest in what is to follow. Don't forget to announce the speaker again by name as you sit down.

Thank-you

When a guest has finished speaking, and the applause has died down, it is customary for a member of the host organization to give a brief thank-you. Again, this is not a speech in its own right. It shows that you have been listening with interest if you can touch on a couple of the points the speaker made which you found particularly fascinating, but this is no time to be contentious or critical. Beware also of making a summary of what you have just heard. This implies either that you think the speaker wasn't clear, or that in your opinion the audience is too stupid to have understood.

If you found the speech extremely dull, you should still thank the speaker warmly. Imagine, it could have been you standing up there, watching people nod off all around you. You could save the speaker a sleepless night of worry if you can find a couple of nice things to say about the speech.

2 PREPARING YOUR SPEECH

So you have been asked to make a speech! You will probably be feeling a mixture of pleasure – because it is certainly an honor to be singled out in this way – and dread: fear of standing up in a roomful of people, with all eyes upon you, and making a mess of it. For ways of calming your nerves, see page 52; to be sure you don't make a mess of it, read on.

You will already have agreed on a date for the event. Make a note in your diary to spend the evening before the event at home, as a wild party could leave you feeling less than ready. On the day of the event you should also avoid a heavy or alcoholic lunch.

Find out as much as you can about the program for the occasion. As you will have gathered from the previous chapter, there are basically two types of speeches, a toast and a response, and the main speech is likely to take the form of a response. Find out which yours is and where it fits in the program if there are several speeches. Find out the subject of the main speech and the identity of the other speakers. And always ask, if you are not told, how long you are expected to speak.

Other points that you will need to know concern the audience. Never lose sight of the fact that your job is to interest and entertain the audience, and that you will need to show them every consideration. Will there be any notables present, such as politicians or other celebrities? What is the average age of the audience, and is it mixed or single sex? What is their purpose in gathering? Are they attending a school reunion or a veterans dinner? How formal is the occasion? Is it a

18

joyful celebration or a solemn commemoration? Will it be white tie, or will everyone dress for a medieval banquet?

Consider why you have been chosen to address the gathering and aim right from the beginning to restrict your speech to that one topic. If you have been asked to introduce the guest speaker, no one will thank you for discussing your expertise in breeding prize-winning zebra finches.

The purpose of your speech

Your job may be simply to pay a tribute or offer a thank-you. On the other hand, it may be to deal with a specific topic. The topic can be chosen or suggested by the guest organization, or it can be left up to you, the speaker.

Consider carefully the purpose of speaking on your chosen topic.

* You may be speaking purely to inform or entertain. Your topic could be something like "How I overcame cancer," or "How I built a replica of the capitol entirely out of matchsticks." You will be telling the audience something they have never heard before, because it is unique to your experience.

* You may be speaking to argue a case, to persuade or convince the audience of the rightness of your point of view. Speeches that fall into this category could be "Why this town needs a bypass," or "Why I should be elected Mayor," or "Why I believe the Earth is flat." The issues may be practical, political or moral. The facts will be accessible to everyone; it is your presentation, your slant on them, which is unique.

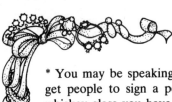

* You may be speaking to urge immediate action: to get people to sign a petition, donate money, buy a whiskey glass you have invented that will float in the bath, or join a political party. You will be aiming to get your audience to participate in a particular way.

Your point of view

If you are trying to sell cordless telephones to the local branch of the farmers' association, your point of view will be that cordless telephones are indispensable to farmers. The thrust of your argument could be entirely positive. If your topic is "How development would ruin this village," your thrust could be entirely negative.

It is, however, probably true that the most interesting speeches are produced when the speaker recognizes both, positive and negative aspects of his topic, discusses them fully, and argues them carefully, finally coming down in favor of one side or the other.

A balanced approach stands a good chance of drawing in people of all schools of thought, whereas a one-sided assessment of a situation could well prompt those who think differently to shut their ears to you altogether.

Preliminary thoughts

Once you have a full picture in your mind of the future event and your role in it, you can begin to think about your topic. Eager as you may be to get the speech down on paper and commit it to memory, you will be jumping the gun if you try to do this immediately. As time passes, new thoughts will inevitably occur to you, and you will either have to restructure your whole speech to get them in, or – even worse – leave them unsaid.

So carry the topic around in your mind for a few

days, and let the ideas sprout spontaneously. Jot down a few notes when you get an idea, so that you can follow it up later if it still seems worthwhile. Keep a notebook and pencil by your bed, because original ideas are most likely to occur to you when your mind is freewheeling rather than concentrating, and you may have your most interesting thoughts just before you fall asleep or on waking up. Another good time for mental freewheeling is while traveling; take a pocket tape recorder with you.

Research

Whatever topic you are going to speak on, you will be well advised to research it as thoroughly as you can. Say it is your pleasant duty to respond to a toast, and you have been allotted five minutes to do so. This is not a big speech, and yet it will benefit from a little diligent research. Find out as much as you can about the person proposing the toast – about his or her career or professional reasons for attending the event, that is – and use this information when you thank him. It will help the audience to put him in context, and he is unlikely to have boasted about his own achievements.

To complete this kind of research, you could apply to the speaker in person for information, but it shows more tact and interest if you use other sources. If the speaker is a local celebrity, the local library or newspaper could help, and you could contact colleagues for more career details. If the speaker is someone from the American Heart Association, then obviously the information you want will be available from them.

If you have been invited to speak on a subject in which you are an expert – say your experience of learning to throw Bizen pots in Japan at the wheel of a master potter – then you should still read up on your subject, as there may be things you have forgotten since you returned from Japan, or new developments in seaweed glazes that you ought to catch up on.

It is absolutely crucial when making a speech that you get all your facts right. If the audience notices that you have made a mistake, their reaction is going to be to wonder how many others you have made that they are unaware of. Don't imagine you can get away with sliding over anything you don't know. The audience will sense that you are bluffing and you will lose credibility.

Finally, remember not to rely so heavily on your research that you exclude your own opinions. The speech is your personal property, and no one wants to hear you paraphrase someone else. The one sure way of making your speech come alive is to inform it with your own views and your own character. That way the audience will know that they are getting something new, something that no one has ever heard before, and not just a pale reflection of something you've read.

TIP

* When considering your topic, ask yourself six questions: who? what? how? when? where? why? The answers to these will give you plenty of meat for your speech.

The speech begins to take shape

After you have allowed time for spontaneous thoughts and done your research, you should be ready to think about the shape of your speech. Read through your notes and see what begins to emerge.

Think of structuring your speech in three parts: an introduction, a development, and a conclusion. Your aim at the beginning of the speech is to grab the audience's attention. Many speakers, especially those who lack confidence, begin by apologizing for what they are about to say. This is a disastrous move, as it will convince the audience that what they are going to hear will not be worth hearing. Think of your introduction as an appetizer for what is to come. It should contain the main thrust of your speech in embryo form. It should pose some questions that call for answers you will hope to provide in the main body of your speech.

The development is the core of your speech. In it your aim will be to make your audience understand and appreciate your point of view. One of the main dangers for speakers here is that they confuse "development" with "digression." As they get into their stride and begin to bask in the power of public speaking, they start

23

to digress from the subject at hand. The audience will become impatient unless they can sense a logical sequence to the points you are making, and this is one good reason for careful structuring and for sticking to the structure once you have planned it.

Another danger during the development of the speech is that you may get carried away by your chosen topic and give the minutest details of the latest research in your field, as if you were speaking to a committee of experts. Bear in mind at all times the need for your audience to be entertained as well as informed. If you quote lists of statistics to them, or speak in mathematical formulae or in jargon that they don't understand, they will grow tired and you will lose their sympathy.

So whatever the length of time you are allotted, keep your development clear, logical, and concise. Unwrap your central theme as if you were peeling the layers from an onion, and you will hold your audience enthralled until you reach your conclusion.

The conclusion is perhaps the hardest part. Even if they don't agree with you, you should leave your audience feeling appreciation for the fresh slant you have brought to the topic, and intrigued and pleased by what they have heard. The purpose of the conclusion is to sum up, and you should stick to doing just that, without being tempted to repeat everything you have already said.

The closing words are always difficult. If your speech is a toast, the problem is solved for you, as long as you remember to end by proposing that everyone drink to it together. For a thank-you, end by reiterating your gratitude. The best ending for other speeches may be a provocative one that will bring a smile to the lips of your audience and a delighted round of applause.

Writing your speech

The next stage is to write your speech in full. Think of this very much as a first draft: if you feel that by putting marks on paper you will be committing yourself, your thoughts will not flow freely. Give yourself plenty of time. Sir Winston Churchill, one of the world's great orators, was once asked if speech-making came naturally to him. He confessed that not only did he find it very hard work, but that sometimes he spent several hours getting just one sentence right. So don't imagine you can leave this vital stage in the preparation of your speech to the very last minute.

Use of language

At this point, don't worry about the finer aspects of polishing your speech; they come later. But before you begin it will be helpful to note one or two things about your use of language. Speech-making is one of the arts of communication, and your first duty is to make yourself understood. So stick to plain English.

Avoid out of date expressions, such as "perchance," or "it behoves me"; avoid slang, as it might not be understood by your audience; and avoid technical jargon for the same reason. Never be tempted to swear, since this will make you more enemies than friends. Clichés are hackneyed and people are so used to

TIPS FOR WRITING BETTER ENGLISH

* Avoid unnecessary qualifying words such as "very," "really," "thoroughly." Statements will be bolder and simpler without them and, as a result, will have much more impact.

* Avoid unnecessary reinforcing words, as in the expressions "brutal rape," "end result," "serious crisis." In each case, the first word is redundant. To say "brutal rape" suggests that rape can be other than brutal.

* Avoid using phrases where one word will do. A current cliché that irritates listeners is "at this point in time." Say "now."

* Don't use a long or elaborate word when a short, simple word will do just as well. Say "about" instead of "approximately," and "know-ledge" instead of "cognizance."

* Speak in the active rather than the passive voice. This means saying "John did something," and not: "Something was done by John." The first form is strong, the second weak.

* Choose words that are positive rather than in the negative. Instead of saying "I did not pass my exam," say: "I failed my exam." Instead of saying "He was not happy with the arrangements," say "He was unhappy with the arrangements."

hearing them that they have become meaningless. For this reason they are as bad as swearing. If you want to describe something, don't use a cliché, and if you want to emphasize something, don't swear. Think out precisely what you mean, and say it in good clear English – an exact and possibly original phrase will have a far greater impact than a worn expletive.

A further important point to remember at this stage is that a speech is meant to be heard and not read. What you write should therefore sound like spoken English. The audience will respond much better if you speak directly to them rather than orating, so try to avoid any literary turns of phrase and use normal conversational English.

Complex sentences that would be perfectly acceptable in a written article will not work now, as the audience won't be able to go back if they've missed something. Nor will obscure or high-flown language be appropriate, as no one in the audience will have brought a dictionary. If you must use a little-known term because it pertains to the subject of your speech, by all means do so, but have the courtesy to explain it to your audience the first time you use it.

Getting the beginning right

The audience will already have formed some ideas about you by the time you get up to speak. The chairman or some other person will have introduced you with a few remarks, and your bearing while you listen to them will have told the audience whether you are relaxed and confident about your speech or nervous and ill at ease.

When you stand up to speak your first words usually address the company quite formally, though if you are a practised speaker, you may begin by making some humorous remark about what the chairman has just said before prefacing the speech with a more formal address.

The address is "Mr. Chairman, ladies and gentlemen," or "Madam Chairwoman, ladies and gentlemen," or "Madam Chairwoman and ladies," according to whichever is appropriate. If the chairperson is a woman, find out in advance how she likes to be addressed – some women hold strong views on this! Any guest of honor who should be mentioned separately follows after the chairman like this: "Mr. Chairman, Mr. Pollock, ladies and gentlemen." Reeling off a long list of celebrities before you get to your speech is tedious, and often it is best to lump V.I.P.s together, like this: "Madam Chairwoman, distinguished guests, ladies and gentlemen." Obviously you will need to use tact and diplomacy in deciding how to begin, and to a certain extent you may take your lead from the previous speakers.

Having addressed your audience, you need to grab their attention immediately and get them interested. You must make them believe that what you are about to tell them will be fascinating, so that they will hang on every word.

GOOD OPENINGS

* Offer your audience results. Outline the problem that faces them, such as the fact that their bowling team has once again come last in the league, and tell them that you have a strategy for winning next year's championship.

* Show your audience that you are just like them. Say that you would never have gotten to design Elizabeth Taylor's wedding bouquet without the inspiring childhood experience of watching the local flower club arrange the holiday flowers.

* Shock them. If you are speaking on behalf of the Cancer Research Society, congratulate the audience on its healthy appearance and then ask if they know that 11 percent of all woman suffer at one time or another from some form of cancer.

* Begin with a vivid personal example of your theme. Tell them about your own dyslexic child's struggles with reading and exams, or tell them how the sight of your grandmother bottling plums inspired you to set up your own international business, marketing natural preserves.

* Amuse them. Begin with a joke or an intriguing historical illustration of their current dilemma.

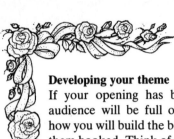

Developing your theme

If your opening has been tantalizing enough, your audience will be full of expectation, waiting to hear how you will build the body of your speech. Try to keep them hooked. Think of your subject as a dark labyrinth through which only you know the way. Imagine that you are leading them through it with a flashlight, illuminating this corner and that as you go. They must keep right behind you or they will get lost, and they must look only where you point the beam.

In order to guide them through your subject, you

HOW TO KEEP THEM LISTENING

* Use logical arguments.

* Build up your evidence step by step.

* Give dramatic illustrations of the points you make.

* Give personal examples wherever you can.

* Be specific.

* Consider opposing points of view.

* Keep everything simple and succinct.

* Avoid boring lists and irrelevant asides.

* Gather your evidence together for the conclusion.

---

must establish a clear and logical sequence to your speech. Link your points with suspense. Remember the technique used by writers of fictional "cliffhangers" and television mini-series, and make them eager for more.

A rousing ending

If you have carried your audience with you to the end, your conclusion should be an inevitable one which they are not surprised to have reached. It will probably take the form of a forceful restatement of the main thrust of your speech, but you could also end by summing up both sides of the argument, perhaps posing a teasing question, and throwing the whole debate open to your audience.

If you are hoping to convert your listeners to a cause or excite them to action, you will surely want to end with a rallying cry. If you have been unraveling a mystery for them, you will put an end to their anticipation with its solution.

If you are proposing a toast or giving thanks, don't forget to end with the suggestion that the assembled company should raise their glasses.

All good speeches take slightly less time than their audience expected. Always finish within a few minutes of your allotted time and never run over it. It is far better to have your listeners disappointed because there is no more than to see them sneaking a look at their watches or craning their necks to see if they can recognize someone else in the audience.

Editing

Once you have a first draft, leave it for a few days, and then read it out aloud to yourself to see what it sounds like and whether it comes naturally to your voice. Put into it all the dramatic feeling that you hope to use on

the occasion, and allow time to look around at the audience, to pause for laughter, etc.

Now ask yourself whether you honestly are happy with it. It would be very unusual if you did not find something to criticize at this stage. Perhaps the words you have chosen don't seem to slip naturally off your tongue. You may have gotten the inflection wrong in a couple of places, and this will alert you to the fact that certain points could be better – or more naturally –

expressed. You may wonder about the logic behind a particular sequence of points, and feel there is a clearer way of expressing what you want to say. A fresh look at the speech after a rest from it will suggest all sorts of questions that you can deal with while editing.

Your job now is to go over the speech, reworking any dubious parts, cutting irrelevancies and padding, and substituting specific words and expressions for vague ones. Never lose sight of the overall shape and clear sense of your speech, and don't forget that you are leading your audience through a labyrinth where the way ahead must be made clear for them.

Check how long it took to read the speech aloud. If you went over your time, you will need to prune it back quite drastically. Look carefully to see where there is any dead wood. Do you give longwinded examples or use ten words where two might do? If, on the other hand, it is too short, you may consider incorporating some more research; but on the whole it is a good idea to finish before your allotted time. Don't pad the speech with extra paragraphs just for the sake of length, or it will lose its punch.

TIPS FOR EDITING YOUR SPEECH

* Be ruthless. Delete everything from your draft that is not relevant to your theme.

* Be honest. Rewrite any passages or sentences that sound unnatural.

* Be precise in your choice of words.

* Work at it until you have got something that runs easily off your tongue.

* Check that it doesn't run over the given time.

* Once you have edited it, read it aloud to yourself again, and make any further adjustments you deem necessary. Keep doing this until you reach your final version. You will know when you have found it, because your speech will now sound as good as you think you can make it.

---

3 HUMOR

People enjoy laughing, and it actually does them good, too. There is a famous true story of a man who was told he had an incurable disease. Though he was in the best hospital, no one could do anything for him. So he decided to cure himself with laughter. He had a VCR in his room, and on this he watched funny films until he ached from laughing. He succeeded in achieving his own cure by literally laughing himself better.

This story illustrates the positive power of laughter, and the art of making people laugh is one of the most effective tools in the speech-maker's bag. A laughing audience is a happy audience, and if the audience is happy, then your speech has been a success.

Humor enlivens any speech. It relaxes the audience and puts them in a good mood. It predisposes them to listen to you and to sympathize with your viewpoint. Laughter is a great leveler, because it shows people that they share the same capacity for enjoyment.

You may be born with a natural talent for making people laugh with an adroit turn of phrase or a droll expression. If you are not, it is never too late to learn.

What is humor?

What is humor? Think of things that make you laugh, and you'll probably agree that humor involves a discrepancy between what is expected and what happens. Take the example of the man who slips on a banana peel. He is going about his normal business when, wham! – he suddenly takes a tumble. When the carpet is jerked out from under someone, everyone laughs. The more pretentious the person, the greater

the fall, and the bigger the laugh.

Thus, the punchline of a joke, or any successful funny remark, relies on a surprizing reversal of what has gone before – a contrast, a contradiction, an incongruity. It is always (potentially) funny when something that's expected to work goes wrong, whether it's a washing machine or a new city plan. And it's also funny when something that's renowned for its failings manages to succeed against all odds: think of an old jalopy overtaking a brand new Porsche on the highway.

Humor can be wry, whimsical, bizarre, affectionate, cynical, sick, blue, malicious, insulting, witty, innocent, or outrageous. Which type you choose to use depends on you and on your view of your audience.

POINTS TO REMEMBER

* People enjoy humor, so don't forget to include some laughs in your speech.

* Humor relaxes your audience; it is also a great leveler.

* The punchline of a joke relies on surprise.

Using humor

An accomplished speaker will not be wracking his brains at the last minute for something funny to say, because he will have a collection of jokes and stories on hand from which to choose.

As soon as you know that you are going to give a speech, start collecting humorous material, even if it

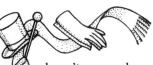

doesn't seem relevant to your topic. Keep a notebook or open a file. Jot down right away the gist of any story or joke you hear or read that appeals to you. You will soon build up quite a collection. Browsing through books of jokes and funny stories will add more material, as will watching comedy shows on the television. Don't be put off by a joke you have heard before – probably few if any of your audience have done so.

When you have written your speech, underline the key points and see if you can adapt any of your jokes to illustrate them. If you can, weave the humor neatly into the narrative, so that it will come as a real surprise.

It's often a good idea as well to make a relevant joke before you get to the main body of your speech, to warm up your audience. Put aside your notes, and deliver the joke as if it had just occurred to you. If your audience's first reaction to you is laughter, you're off to a good start.

Don't get carried away

Some speakers get so carried away with their own jokes that they lose sight of the reason they were asked to speak in the first place. You probably haven't been hired as a stand-up comedian, but with some other purpose in mind. Don't let your message get submerged under a welter of one-liners and funny stories.

Anyway, a stream of gags is tiring for an audience. If you are trying too consciously for a laugh, they will begin to feel obligated to guffaw every time you pause for breath, and their face muscles will start to ache. Jokes are much funnier if they unexpectedly punctuate serious matter than if they are fired off relentlessly, one after the other.

Consider your audience

Always consider your audience before deciding on the type of humor you want to use. Remember your purpose is to make them enjoy themselves, and you won't succeed in doing this if they find your jokes crass or offensive. Even if only one or two people in the crowd finds a joke distasteful, it can ruin the atmosphere for the rest of your speech. So steer well clear of religious jokes, and be very careful when using sexual humor. Some sexual (as opposed to sexist) jokes can be very funny, but don't run the risk if you are speaking to an audience known for its piety, or to a group of people of the opposite sex, or to people from other countries.

If you want to tell a genuinely funny, not crass, sexual joke to a tolerant gathering, do so by all means. But unless you know them well, wait to hear how they respond to the jokes of the speakers who precede you before making your final decision. If they laugh at risqué humor, you should be fairly safe to include it; if they laugh tentatively or sit stony-faced, leave it out.

Aim your jokes well

Jokes are often told about or against people or attitudes. You might hear a joke about an Irishman or against the conservation movement. You can make your jokes relevant to the occasion by choosing as the butt of the joke a person or a subject familiar to your audience. It is easy enough to adapt a joke by substituting the relevant name or term – a joke about some health food fads or a current political figure well known to your audience.

You can do this more successfully if you have found out beforehand something about the most pressing

37

concerns of the group you will be speaking to. They may be an activist group that has had a run-in with the local congressman. In that case, no doubt a joke about that congressman would go down very well. It would relax the audience, because they would feel instantly that you share their reservations about the congress-man and that you sympathize with them.

Always be very careful when making individuals in the audience or the audience as a whole the butt of your joke. This works only if it is done very good-naturedly; if it misfires, it can cause deep suspicion and offense. If you want to make gentle fun of them, they will react better if you have first made fun of yourself. Making jokes at your own expense is a sure-fire way to get any audience to like you.

Delivery

A good joke can fall flat on its face if the delivery is wrong. There are two basic things to consider when delivering a joke: your own attitude and the way you express and the pace at which you deliver the joke – your timing.

The importance of confidence
If you are afraid the audience won't think your joke funny, you will probably look timid and worried as you are telling it. If your voice is quaking and your body cramped, your audience will not be prepared to respond with a huge belly laugh, and so no matter how funny the joke is, you'll probably raise only a titter.

If, on the other hand, you approach them with a knowing smile and confidence in your bearing, they will already be alerted to the fact that you are about to make them laugh, and they will smile in anticipation. If you put the right expression into your delivery, you could have them rocking to and fro in their seats with tears streaming down their cheeks, before you even say anything very funny.

To get the right degree of confidence, you need to pick an appropriate joke, which you yourself find funny, and to rehearse it well. With a little practice, you will discover which jokes get the best response, and you can earmark these for use at the beginning and during the early part of your speech, trying out new additions to your repertory later on. It really does not

---

TIPS FOR USING HUMOR

* Make a collection of funny stories and jokes.

* Begin with a really good joke to warm up the audience.

* Don't get carried away delivering a stream of gags that are unrelated to your chosen topic.

* Consider your audience and never tell an offensive or hurtful joke.

* Make the butt of your joke a subject or person familiar to the audience.

* Laugh with them, not at them.

* A joke at your own expense will always raise a laugh.

---

matter if some members of the audience have heard the joke before; as long as it is funny and well told, they will be prepared to laugh at it each time they hear it.

Timing
Good timing is essential for successful joke delivery. Don't gabble it all at once – it will sound as though you think it's so terrible you can't wait to get to the end. Make sure everyone can hear and understand what you are saying. Make good use of the dramatic pause to build up suspense, and hold the pause for a little longer than normal before delivering the punchline. If the audience gets the feel and rhythm of what you are saying, they'll be even more ready to laugh heartily at your joke when the time comes.

Timing also has to do with stress and expression. Put your stress on the key words of the joke and accompany them with plenty of expression, on your face as well as in your voice. If you look sneaky, as if you were sharing a secret, or wicked, or fresh, or roll your eyes, your joke will raise much more of a laugh than if you stand there with a straight face, reciting it in a monotone.

TIPS ON GOOD DELIVERY

* A confident delivery makes all the difference.

* Practice good timing.

* Practice putting lots of expression into your jokes.

The awful possibility of failure

Every public speaker like every other entertainer, has nights when his jokes fall flat and his audience just doesn't respond. It's not a pleasant feeling the first time this happens to you, but if you are an experienced speaker, confident of your own ability, you will be able to accept the odd failure philosophically, in the knowledge that success comes much more often.

If the audience is sitting glumly, with not the slightest suspicion of a smile at your funniest joke, you can either keep trying with your humor or you can give up on it. If you decide to risk another joke, chortle to yourself after you've delivered the punchline even if they remain silent, just to show you're still enjoying yourself. Another way of calling their bluff is to introduce the joke by saying, "As Bob Hope once remarked . . . " – this lays the responsibility for the joke fairly and squarely on a bona-fide comedian, so the audience can't blame you if it's not funny.

The easiest jokes to get away with are one-liners, because if no one laughs, you can move on quickly without losing face. But if you are telling a story with a long build-up to the punchline, and that falls flat, it can leave you with an empty silence on your hands. You can try to remedy the matter by turning the joke against yourself, as a teller of jokes that fall flat, but if that in turn fails to raise a laugh, you're in even deeper trouble than before.

Lengthy stories can be difficult to remember, and from telling jokes to friends everyone knows the anguish of seeing expectant faces freeze as you forget the punchline. Among people you know well this doesn't matter; it can even be mildly amusing to build up a reputation for being the person who can never

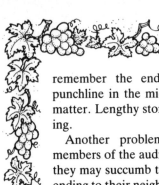

remember the end of a joke. But to forget the punchline in the middle of a public speech is another matter. Lengthy stories always need thorough rehearsing.

Another problem with stories is that if some members of the audience have heard your joke before, they may succumb to the temptation of whispering the ending to their neighbors. So then a good proportion of your listeners will merely nod their heads with smug self-satisfaction when you get to the punchline. With short jokes and one-liners that may be already familiar, this is not a problem as there is no time to spoil the joke by whispering, and a good delivery will in any case guarantee a laugh, even from someone who has heard it before.

It's good to kick off with a couple of jokes that always go down well, and build up gradually to a long story. By the time you reach it, you should have an idea of whether your audience will find it funny or not, and if you think there's a chance they won't like it, you can leave it out.

IF THEY DON'T LIKE YOUR JOKES....

* Show you think your jokes are funny, even if no one else does.

* One-liners are safer bets than lengthy stories.

* Gauge the sense of humor of your audience by their response to the jokes of previous speakers.

* Leave out any jokes you think won't appeal.

---

4 GETTING INTO GEAR

Your speech is prepared and rehearsed. You have the confidence of knowing that your subject has been well researched and that what you have written has a clear structure, is in good English, informative, entertaining, even funny in parts. Despite all this, as the day draws closer you are overtaken by a terrible anxiety that everything could go wrong. Will your mind go blank as you rise to speak? Will your audience sit stony-faced or laugh with derision as you stumble over your opening remarks? Will those at the back be able to hear? And what sort of impression will you create? Will people fidget and snore, or do you see them in your mind's eye leaping to their feet to give you a standing ovation?

As all these possibilities and more rush through your imagination; now is the time to take stock, calm your nerves, and assess your best chance for a creditable performance.

Nerves

Nerves are every speaker's worst enemy. All public performers – actors and actresses, television announcers and interviewers, chairmen at board meetings, and even the most experienced speakers – suffer from stage fright, but with practice this debilitating affliction can be overcome. There will probably never be a time when you stand up to speak completely free of nerves, and in fact this is a good thing, because if a performer is completely relaxed, the performance will lack dynamism and will fail to interest the audience.

Being keyed up, excited and tense before your

43

speech means that your mental faculties will be on the alert, you will radiate energy and rivet the attention of your listeners. But for an after-dinner speaker, there is a lot of the evening to get through before you even make your opening remarks: pleasantries and introductions and conversation over the dinner, not to mention the food and drink you will be expected to consume.

If you are nervous to the point of not being able to concentrate on anything but the ordeal to come, you will communicate your anxiety to the people around you. They will be as worried about your speech as you are, which is not a good way to start.

So before you start out for your speaking engagement, examine your nervous state quite candidly, as if you were an interested outside observer, and take some steps to soothe the worst of your fears.

Physical symptoms of nerves
What are the primary physical manifestations of nervousness? Your brain is probably sending signals of fear to your body that are as urgent as if you were about to face a den of ravenous lions rather than a sympathetic audience.

You will probably have adopted the hunched posture of someone who stands in peril of his life: a stooped back, rounded shoulders, lowered head, rigid neck, and clenched muscles. Relax! You will certainly come out of it alive, and if you can convince your body of this fact, you should be able to adopt a normal posture, upright but easy.

The hunched posture of fear protects the front of the body – the most vulnerable part, where you expect to be hit by your enemy (the audience) – and it caves in the chest and lungs, which need to be open and free if you are to speak well. If you are nervous, your breathing will be shallow and short, you will not be taking in enough oxygen, and your brain will feel blinkered by fear. Deep-breathing exercises are the answer to this problem.

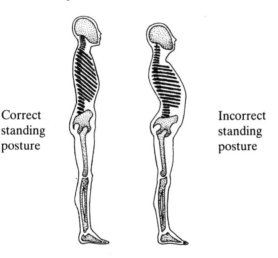

Correct standing posture

Incorrect standing posture

Stand erect with your head up and shoulders back. Pull in your bottom without consciously thrusting out your chest; your spine should form a straight line all the way from the base of your skull to your coccyx. Breathe in slowly and fully to fill your lungs to capacity, then exhale slowly. Repeat this until you feel calmer. Keep breathing deeply, though not in such an exaggerated way, until you deliver your speech, and remember to keep a good posture.

Nerves are also likely to make your palms sweat. It's an unpleasant feeling and particularly unwelcome in a situation where you will be called upon to shake hands with numerous people. Sweating is another "fight or flight" reaction. Deep breathing to calm your nerves will help, and so will working off your energy by running around the block. In fact, it would be a good idea to walk the last stretch of your journey to the meeting room, establishing a strong steady rhythm, breathing deeply, and thinking over your speech as you do so. But just in case you're still perspiring, carry a large handkerchief – you can always go to the restroom to mop your forehead.

What is it that scares you?

You might think this is an unnecessary question. You are, of course, terrified of making a fool of yourself. But wait a moment: are you in the habit of making a fool of yourself? Certainly not. Then why are you afraid that you will lose control on this particular occasion? You know exactly what you are going to say, and you are confident that it is worth hearing. Surely this should put you in command of the situation. But it's not the speech itself that has pulverized your nerves: it's the thought of standing up in front of all those faces – a sea of pale, expectant blobs lifted toward you, a mass of eyes pinned to you, under which you fear fading into a shadow of yourself, fumbling with your notes, and mutely opening and closing your mouth.

The thought of it makes your mouth dry, because it feels like an inquisition. It's you against them, and they are bound to win because of their great numbers.

You might begin to feel a little better as soon as you have admitted your secret fears, because they do have

46

THE ALEXANDER TECHNIQUE

Frederick Matthias Alexander (1869–1955) was born in Tasmania, Australia, and grew up with an ambition to become a Shakespearean orator. Despite suffering respiratory problems, he went to work for a dramatic company in Melbourne, but was then struck by bouts of hoarseness and complete loss of voice. Suspecting that his disability might be self-induced, he spent months observing himself at work in a mirror, and discovered that the way he pulled his head back when speaking was leading to constriction of the larynx which led to hoarseness.

He worked out a method of "primary control," which was to "let the neck be free and let the head be forward and up, and the back widen and lengthen." This was clearly the solution, but he found it was not easy to put it into practice, as his instinct was always to revert to his old bad habits. He had to develop "conscious constructive control."

Once he had achieved this, he discovered that his respiratory problems disappeared along with the hoarseness, and he went to London to teach his technique to others. His methods made a great impact, and among his most famous pupils were George Bernard Shaw and Aldous Huxley.

The Alexander Institute in London trains teachers who work all over Britain. The technique is of particular help to those who use their voice in their profession, such as singers and actors as well as speakers.

their ludicrous aspect. If your subject is very explosive or your audience very drunk, there is a chance you may be met with hostility, but under normal circumstances invited speakers have the best possible audience. They are relaxed and friendly, and their good spirits make them encouraging and supportive rather than critical and restless.

As you rise to address them, their eyes are not going to be drilling menacingly into you, discovering your inner weaknesses and faults. Your speech is, after all, not being forced on them: they have all come to the event knowing they are going to hear it. For all you know, they may be genuinely looking forward to it. Although, as they fall silent to hear your opening remarks, their eyes will certainly be upon you, their mood will not be hostile, but welcoming, expectant, and curious. All you have to do is give a reasonable performance – and not speak for too long – and they will reward you with warm applause.

If logic has not convinced you that you have no course for fear, think further. Instead of imagining your audience's eyes drilling into you, put yourself, in your imagination, into a position of command. You are going to be the only one standing up – they will all be sitting down. You will speak; they will be silent. Think of yourself as the giver, the active one, and of them as passive recipients. Now see what power you wield. If you doubt it, envision pointing to someone in the audience and saying, "You, over there in the spotted bow tie, what do you think about all this?" And then the poor man in the spotted tie will be in the hot seat, with everybody staring at him. Do you imagine he would acquit himself any better than you? This is just one of a number of ways in which you can build up confidence.

If the very idea of diverting the audience's attention from your face to someone else's makes you feel relieved, why not employ this as a device at the beginning of your speech to take the pressure off yourself and allow you to relax? A public speaker does not usually produce visual aids, like maps, charts etc., but there may be some object that you could bring along and arrange to have placed on the table in front of you if it's small, or on a side table nearby if large, to which you could refer.

You might then begin "Ladies and gentleman, I ask you to look at this piece of Roman pottery/policeman's hat/fine ceiling [the choice, of course, depending on the place], and consider ..." Their eyes will be instantly away from you and your voice will have a good chance of getting off to a normal start.

What is the worst that could happen?

If you are making an informative speech yourself, the chances are that you have already attended gatherings at which other people have spoken. It will be useful to ask yourself about the worst speech you ever heard. It was probably either embarrassing, because crass and in bad taste, or irrelevant to the topic that was supposed to be under discussion. Now, you know, because you have prepared your speech well, that yours falls into neither of these categories.

Realistically speaking, your speech will be, at the very worst, boring. You have probably heard many boring speeches, and you may have noticed that they have one redeeming factor in common: they are quickly forgotten. The speaker may have labored painstakingly for weeks over something so dull that its sentences make no impression whatever on the minds of the listeners. They will probably have forgotten what was

said in his opening remarks before the end of the piece.

So don't worry if your carefully prepared speech causes eyes to glaze and bottoms to squirm, not one of your audience will be lying awake in bed that night smirking over your faulty sentence construction in the third paragraph or disagreeing with your interpretation of statistics in the twenty-sixth. Each and every one will be sound asleep. And no one will hold it against you for being a boring speaker as long as you remember to keep your speech short.

Other pitfalls for the nervous

The opening is usually the worst part. So instead of beginning with a brilliant, convoluted sentence that shows off the sparkling caliber of your mental faculties, but which in the circumstances is likely to trip you up and befuddle your audience, why not kick off in a conversational mode? Every athlete needs a warm-up period before doing his very best, and that's true of speakers too. Once you have passed the first sentence, the next will follow more easily, and soon you will start enjoying yourself.

Just occasionally, however, a speaker may get distracted later in the speech, stumble over the words, suffer an onslaught of nerves, look up and suddenly see the audience bearing down without mercy. The words will just dry up. Nothing could be worse. It's wise to be prepared for this. Good notes will help (page 68). But what you need most is to take a deep breath, put your audience back in perspective (they were enjoying what you were saying and are waiting for you to continue), and plunge right back in. You might have a joke or some aside planned for getting over an awkward moment, such as someone knocking over a wine bottle or a waiter dropping a tray full of plates, and such a device will ease tension all over the room and probably earn you a laugh as well.

Some people resort to liquor to calm their nerves. Beware! This can do more harm than good. If the speech is to be delivered at a dinner there will probably be plenty to drink – cocktails before the meal, wine (possibly several wines) with the meal, and a liqueur afterward. If your throat has gone dry, stick to seltzer water, and make sure you have a full glass of it ready when you stand up to speak – as well as something with which to give the toast. You can sip water too during pauses in your speech: sip alcohol while you speak and you'll give the impression of being desperate. Try to restrict yourself to only one drink before you rise. It will stimulate and relax you, whereas several drinks will slow your thought processes, make your gestures clumsy, and slur your speech. Don't eat too much, however delicious the food; this too could slow down your thoughts, or perhaps give you indigestion.

The last pitfall of the evening that awaits the nervous speaker is one that you won't have contemplated at all. When applause has greeted your final words and you have sat down, you may feel so relieved to have acquitted yourself well that your pent-up nerves suddenly burst the dam of your inhibitions, and you become extremely talkative. Watch yourself for signs of overexcitement and try not to get too carried away. You may feel an urgent craving for food, especially if your knotted stomach would not let you eat earlier, and the temptation to down a drink in euphoric celebration may be overwhelming. Try to moderate your behavior until you get home. Then you can fling your arms around and shout as loud as you like.

TIPS FOR CONQUERING NERVES

* Do deep-breathing exercises or run around the block. Walk to the meeting room.

* Think of yourself as being in control, the one with the power, and don't for a minute let your audience dominate you in your imagination.

* Don't try to conquer nerves with alcohol. One drink is fine, more is probably too many. You'll need your wits about you.

* Begin in a conversational mode rather than with a vastly complicated and brilliant sentence.

* Use your nervous tension to give your speech energy and dynamism.

* The best thing you can do for your audience is to please them; the worst thing they can do to you is to forget you – and that's not so bad.

* Find out beforehand as much as you can about the occasion, the location, and the audience.

* Remember that all speakers, even the very best, suffer regularly from nerves.

Your relationship with the audience

Ideally, you will have your audience with you all the way. This doesn't necessarily mean that they agree with everything you say, but that they are listening, following, thinking things through – above all that they feel empathy with you. If you gain your audience's interest and respect, so that they are receptive and welcoming to what you say, half your battle is won already. So how do you go about winning over an audience?

Let's start by assuming that they are disposed to like you. Most of these audiences, after all, have come to enjoy the occasion. (For how to deal with an audience that is not so well disposed, see page 77.) The most essential requirement for making them positively warm to you is to show your listeners every consideration.

Consideration for your listeners

Begin by getting to your feet in a positive manner, which will give them the impression that you have got something to tell them that's worth hearing and that you are looking forward to sharing it with them. If you drag yourself up from your seat and lean against the table, hanging your head, your audience will feel sorry for you before you have even opened your mouth – and pity is not a reaction you should be looking for.

Allow them to hear what you say. Speak clearly, pausing in appropriate places. Don't mumble or ramble. If you make them laugh, wait for their laughter to die down before you resume speaking. If you press ahead, they'll miss something, and it will discourage them from laughing again.

Any audience can be easily distracted. Avoid irritating mannerisms and verbal ticks, such as constant "ums" and "ahs" and constant repetitions of senseless words and phrases. Don't you remember the day you sat in the classroom and counted the number of times the music teacher said "sort of"? The record then was 27. Don't try to beat it.

Allow your audience to follow your train of thought by making your points clearly and linking them logically. Summarize things you've said before regularly rather than expecting them to remember every word you have said. As you probably remember from your own experience, prolonged and sustained listening to one person is quite a strain, however entertaining they might be, so give your audience all the help you can. One sure way of doing this is to use the language of normal speech, casting aside any temptation to launch into grandiose overblown phrases and long, learned words. Remember your audience has just eaten their dinner. Don't let your speech give them indigestion.

Where to look
Bear in mind that public speaking is not like a stage performance. You are not up there alone under the spotlight, orating into a vacuum, with your audience plunged in blackness beneath you. You are in a fully lit room. You can see their faces and read their expressions. You are one of them, and their reactions are part of your speech. Though the occasion may be a formal one, it is still not impersonal.

The question the beginner will want to ask is: where on earth do you look? Accomplished speakers will be able to look at their audience, letting their eyes rest on individuals within it, which will give them the feeling of participation. This is what you are aiming for, but few speakers can achieve it without some practice.

When you rise to your feet, you will be facing your audience, but you are given an immediate break from deciding where to look because the formal address (page 28) obliges you to turn to the chairman or other special guests. By the time this has been completed, you will already be feeling steadier on your legs.

The best way to begin is without making direct eye contact with the audience. Look straight out ahead of you, though not stiffly, and somewhere just above your audience's heads. Don't focus on an object on the wall, or if you do, don't let your eyes stay there too long: heads may turn to see what you're looking at. Keep your eyes focused in mid-air, and concentrate on what you are saying rather than on your audience. As the familiar pattern of your speech begins to develop and you gain confidence, look to either side of you so that you gradually encompass the room, still keeping your eyes above the audience and focused in mid-air.

Now you can begin slowly to draw your listeners in, by focusing on small groups – perhaps half a dozen

people – in turn. As you do this, you will begin to notice people's expressions and whether they are friendly or frowning. The last stage of your growing contact with the audience is to use their reactions to help you. Focus on a friendly person if you need encouragement, or on a frowning person to reinforce emphatic points or offer conciliatory ones.

Beware of making eye contact with individuals too early in your speech. Eyes are extremely powerful and persuasive, and if the person you have chosen returns your stare, you may find it almost impossible to tear your eyes away from him: like weasel and rabbit, you could be locked in each other's gaze to the end.

A courteous speaker will also from time to time turn and look directly at the chairman and important guests.

Talking "to" your audience
The whole point of talking to your assembled audience is to communicate your ideas to them, and to do this you have to be speaking the same language. This means using the words, phrases, and sentence lengths that you would employ in everyday speech: it means being your normal self. All too often, public speakers completely lose sight of the fact that they are talking "to" their audience, and begin to talk "at" them, "over" them, or "down to" them.

You are not giving a lecture at Harvard University. You are not trying to overwhelm people with your brilliance. And you are not speaking to a bunch of five-year-olds. Avoid over-elaborate expressions and obscure words, but don't patronize your audience either, by assuming they know nothing. One of the worst mistakes you can make is to underestimate the intelligence of your listeners. As soon as they realize what you think of them – which will be pretty quickly –

the knowledge that you regard them as nincompoops will infuriate them, and they will be hostile to everything you say.

When in doubt, tread a middle path. Introduce something you think they ought to know about by saying, "Many of you will remember reading about so-and-so in the summer of last year." Gauge the amount of explanation necessary according to the company you are in. If you're addressing the Gardening Club they'll expect to hear some Latin plant names; if you're addressing the Tennis Club, they won't. If you find you're doing too much explaining, it probably means you are talking about the wrong subject, or at least talking about it in the wrong way.

If you are talking "to" your audience, you should be able to strike up a good rapport with them immediately. Use humor (page 34) and good temper to show your sympathy and understanding, and to gain theirs. If the occasion celebrates a milestone in the life of a particular organization, such as the raising of a sum of money for a charitable cause, you can immediately get the audience on your side by praising their efforts. Take time in advance to find out as much as you can about what has been going on, mention a few individual names, and look at the right people as you describe their contributions. But make sure your praise is not too fulsome by inserting an assessment as well, and keep your comments to the achievements of the people concerned and away from their physical attributes.

57

TIPS FOR GOOD AUDIENCE RELATIONS

* Be considerate in the way you speak: make sure you can be heard and understood.

* Don't cause irritation with annoying mannerisms and verbal tics.

* Use humor and good temper to show your sympathy and gain theirs.

* Gradually establish eye contact without allowing yourself to become mesmerized.

* Use normal everyday language.

* Talk "to" your listeners, not "at," "over," or "down to" them.

Checking the arrangements

Public speaking is one of the performing arts, and giving a speech is a lot like acting in a theater in the round, where there is a close contact with the audience. Like any other performers, public speakers should make sure that all aspects of the show in which they are going to take part will run smoothly. It can't be stressed strongly enough that proper attention to practicalities will reward you time after time with the assurance that there will be no last-minute mishaps, and the confidence that the stage has been perfectly set for a good performance.

Correct dress
Make sure you know whether evening or more casual daytime clothes are required for the occasion, and dress accordingly. It's easy enough to check this out by looking at your invitation or ticket, but since you are speaking, you may not have been sent one of these, so call the organizers and find out from them.

Whatever your own preference in clothes, you should pay your hosts and their guests the compliment of dressing to fit in with the occasion. Don't forget that you will succeed only if you strike up a good relationship with your audience, and they won't take kindly to you if they have gone to a lot of trouble and expense with their clothes and you turn up in jeans after a day under the car. You may feel you want to make a political statement by appearing dressed from the ragbag, but this won't do anything except create hostility. Far better to weave the political truth, as you see it, into your speech.

There is a danger, too, in overdressing. If you arrive in the family jewels or clanking with rows of medals, you could run the risk of making your audience feel drab and dowdy. And if you come in full Highland dress complete with kilt and sporran, or in a cerise silk

gown that makes you look like Joan Collins, the chances are that the audience will be so fascinated with your clothes and accessories that they won't listen to a word you say.

So play it smart, dress fashionably but not too flashily, and let the emphasis be on your words and not on your appearance.

Good timekeeping

Good timekeeping is crucial. Two aspects of timekeeping will concern you particularly: the time of your arrival and the length of your speech. You will have agreed on the length of your speech beforehand and written it accordingly, but sometimes arrangements change at the very last moment, and there could be a problem if you are not notified until you get to the meeting. So for safety's sake, phone to check the day before.

If your time has been cut, you will already have earmarked paragraphs that you can trim, and this should now be put into operation. Make sure you run through the shortened speech several times to get used to it, since if you've learned it practically by heart you might give the extended version by mistake. If by any chance you are asked to extend your speech, refuse firmly but politely. The effect of your careful planning will be lost if you pump up your speech with padding or introduce new subjects with which you are not familiar.

Now to the other point. Obviously, you and your hosts will feel anxious if you arrive late, so plan to get to the meeting with plenty of time to spare. If it's your first visit to the place concerned and you are worried about how long to allow for your journey, it might be wise to make the trip a few days beforehand and in the same conditions (rush-hour traffic, perhaps) that you expect to meet at the time.

Your first duty on arrival is to greet your hosts, to set their minds at rest that you haven't been delayed. Then try to take a look at the room in which you will be giving the speech.

The room

It's important to get the feel of the room where you will be giving your speech, so try to find an opportunity to check the arrangements. Find your chair and go and stand behind it to imagine what you will feel like as you rise to your feet later on. Will everyone be able to see you? If not, now is the time to request a change, or at least to make sure that you can stand somewhere else, where you will be seen, to deliver the speech.

If you are standing away from the table, you will probably be offered a lectern: make sure you feel comfortable standing behind it, that it is the right height, and that it faces in exactly the right direction. Walk to it once or twice from your seat, making sure that there are no wires or planters on the way for you to trip over. If you have no lectern, decide in advance where you will put your notes. Are you going to hold

61

them, or will you prop them up against a glass? Make sure the prop is firm enough and that there is no danger of spilling wine on your neighbors.

The sound system
Now is the time to check out the sound system, if there is one. There is nothing more likely to put an audience on edge than the speaker fiddling with a screeching microphone at the last minute. Check that the height of the microphone is right for you, and that the sound is true, and neither too loud nor too soft. Familiarize yourself with the on/off switch, practice using it a few times, and then remind yourself to leave it alone while you speak. If you start fiddling with it, the effect could be very disconcerting for your audience.

The formalities
It is always worthwhile to make a last-minute check of the program to see that your speech is listed with the correct title. If you have prepared a speech on Intensive v. Organic Farming and you are down to speak on Buddhism in Thailand, you may have a little explaining to do when the time comes.

Check the program, too, for the names of all the distinguished guests, and double check that all the people named will actually attend. Don't forget that courtesy demands a preamble to your speech, along the lines of "Mr. Chairman, distinguished guests, ladies and gentlemen" (see page 28). If you are to be the first person to speak, find out if there are any guests who need to be named in the preamble, and make sure that you know how to pronounce their names. If your speech comes later in the evening, you can take your lead from the other speakers.

One formality that you should always observe

62

scrupulously is the golden rule of not over-indulging. In order to keep a clear head, avoid drinking at lunchtime on the day of your engagement, and exercise great restraint during the proceedings if alcohol is available. The key to your success is to be able to rise above the situation and control it, not let it control you, and so the first essential is self-control.

TIPS FOR FINAL ARRANGEMENTS

* Dress correctly. Don't let your clothes push your speech from center stage.

* Speak for the allotted time.

* Be punctual.

* Check out the arrangements in the room.

* Test the sound system yourself.

* Check the details on the program to make sure your speech is correctly titled.

5 DELIVERY

The best speakers are the ones who take control of their audience from the moment they open their mouths. The confident bearing and easy manner of a good speaker have an instantly reassuring effect on the listeners. They will sit back, ready to enjoy themselves.

Taking control does not mean dominating. Think of yourself as a guide rather than a dictator and you will be met with trust. A speaker who wants to force points across by snarling aggressively and fist-shaking will antagonize the audience before they have had time to consider the argument.

A good speaker is like a good actor who has rehearsed the part thoroughly and knows how to use his voice to tease, cajole, sympathize, amuse and impress. Good speakers will know how to breathe, when to pause, what gestures to make. They will know how to use suspense and drama. All these skills will enable them to hold the audience in the palm of their hand.

TIPS FOR TAKING CONTROL

* Never apologize or excuse yourself.

* Never thank the audience for listening. It is their job to thank you!

Reciting from memory or reading from notes?

Before you consider such aspects of delivering your speech as voice, timing, bearing, and coping with distractions, you will have to make a decision about how far you want to commit the speech to memory. You have four options:

1. To read every word of the speech;
2. To commit the speech to memory and recite every word of it;
3. To familiarize yourself with the speech, then deliver it more or less spontaneously;
4. To commit it to memory and use notes to prompt yourself.

Reading your speech

The first option leaves little room for maneuver. It could be awkward, for example, if you have to shout your first sentence, "What a delight it is to be in the company of so many healthy nonagenarians," above the noise of one of the group succumbing to a sudden fit of coughing. A relaxed speaker will allow some leeway to deal with unexpected events such as this, and will also be able to make a few impromptu remarks on the chairman's flattering introduction.

Reading every word of a speech can sound less than lively, especially if the speaker is struggling to decipher his or her own writing. To be faced with someone looking at a piece of paper is not as interesting for the audience as having that person involve them in the

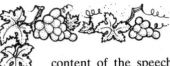

content of the speech, by eye contact and by being aware of their reactions.

However, if you are making your first speech, you may indeed decide that the safest option is to read it in full. You can still make it sound interesting if you memorize it fully enough to be aware of the rhythm and cadences of the sentences, so that you can deliver it in a dramatic manner, looking up at your audience at appropriate points and pausing to let them digest what you are saying, or to allow them to laugh.

Reciting every word

This method has similar disadvantages to the ones described above. The speaker may give the appearance of talking off-the-cuff because there are no notes, but in reality he or she is sticking slavishly to the prepared text. Now, there is nothing wrong with sticking to the text – this is after all, why you have spent so much time choosing the right words and phrases – but the danger of reciting a speech is that you are going to sound like an actor at an audition. If you are concentrating so hard on the words in your head that you forget to communicate with the audience, this method is no better than reading your speech with your head buried in a sheaf of papers.

However, if you are a good actor, it is the method that will come most naturally to you. If you have confidence that your memory won't fail you at the last moment, you can afford to preface your speech with some spontaneous remarks. And you can break off to make a joke if someone knocks over a plant or a burglar alarm goes off outside, in the sure knowledge that you'll be able to pick up where you left off once the disturbance is over.

"Spontaneous" delivery

A practiced speaker will be absolutely at home with the idea of writing a speech, studying it thoroughly, then delivering it without notes and without reciting it word by word. This technique is not to be attempted by the novice.

There are two major pitfalls. The first is that you forget the drift of your speech and end up making rambling digressions, and the second is that the speech in its impromptu rendition is less effective due to the imprecision of its vocabulary. It is a shame to hone and polish your speech, and then at the event to put it away and paraphrase it so that you deliver a pale version of the original.

"Spontaneous" delivery is probably quite all right for celebrities and politicians, who spend half their time making speeches and who have an urbane, smooth, and polished manner. Indeed, it can be used very effectively if the speaker wants to give an impression of smoothness and urbanity, and is more eager to be remembered by the audience for this than for the content of the speech.

It is probably also not such a bad method if you are at a gathering of people you know well and the message of your speech is a simple one, such as thanks or congratulations. But on the whole, it is not a method to be employed if you are a newcomer to public speaking and you want to communicate a set of well-reasoned ideas to the audience to the best of your ability.

Using notes to prompt yourself

This method is a compromise used by many public speakers. After you have written your speech, make a list of the key points, which will help you to remember everything you have written. Write them down – just one word for each – in bold letters on a series of cards (blank index cards are ideal) and number them in order.

Familiarize yourself with your speech so that you have almost completely committed it to memory, but use the cards as reminders, so that if you go blank, you will be able to get back into the swing without anyone noticing you falter.

Cards have the advantage giving you something to hold – and so stop you fiddling with your tie or jewelry –and yet do not flap and crumple up like paper. Cards look extremely professional; they can be kept in your pocket or bag until wanted, and when you slip the front one to the back, you can make a natural pause to look around at your audience. In fact, this method provides you with a chance to take refuge from the audience if you get stuck, and at the same time offers you maximum opportunity for engaging with them.

TIPS

* Don't let your concentration on the words come between you and the audience. Remember you are communicating with them, not taking part in a public-speaking competition.

* Keep your delivery lively.

* Be flexible so that you can make spontaneous remarks.

Movement and gesture

Most of us naturally use our hands when we talk, but as soon as someone gets up to speak in front of an audience for the first time, gestures tend to become cramped and hands an embarrassment.

Where *do* you put your hands when you give a speech? If you are holding a set of prompt cards (see above) or a microphone, one hand is taken care of. Try not to cling to either as if it's the only thing that will save you from drowning. But say you are holding neither? Some speakers clasp their hands modestly in front of them, as if they were preparing to pray, while others clasp their hands behind their back in a military "at ease" pose. There are those who shove their hands in their pockets where they take on a life of their own, jingling coins and car keys in a very irritating manner.

Ideally, your hands should feel free to hang loosely at your sides or to gesture naturally when appropriate. This may sound easy, but, in fact, it takes some practice to achieve.

Practice in front of a mirror

Go and stand in front of a full-length mirror and run through your speech, paying particular attention to your hands. You will soon find out where you need to make gestures. Here are some examples.

* If you are making an emphatic point, such as "We must not let the town council get away with this any longer," you will tend to pound or pump your fist.

* If you are making a statement about distance, "Right across the Appalachian Mountains," you may wish to make an expansive sweeping gesture with your arm.

* If you are posing a question, "So what did they do about it?", you could find yourself raising both hands, palms up, and shrugging.

* If you are weighing something up, "On the one hand, the local community got rich, but on the other, they began to lose their traditional skills," your hands could move like a balance, testing the merits of each issue.

It is important to make use of these and other gestures to illustrate and enliven your speech. At first, as you watch yourself, you will feel awkward, as though you are learning gestures for the first time that should come naturally. Notice where your gestures come from. Do you hold your arms close to your body, with your elbows clamped in so that only your forearms and hands move? If so, you will feel cramped and hemmed in. Let your arms move from the shoulder, give your hands a wider scope, and allow your hips and head to move, too. As you give yourself more freedom, your face will start to express what you feel, so that your

whole personality comes across.

Beware of going to the other extreme and gesticulating wildly all the time for no apparent reason. Someone who throws his hands around constantly is only going to distract the audience from what he is saying. Similarly, be careful to avoid irritating, idiosyncratic gestures, such as tapping your head and whirling your fingers around your ears to indicate thought processes, or repeatedly scratching your nose. You should be able to spot these habits in the mirror and begin to correct them.

Standing still

If you allow yourself to gesture naturally, you won't be standing completely still all the time. But it is not a good idea to pace up and down while you are speaking, because the audience will get tired of watching you pace the room, and they may well begin to concentrate more on your perambulations than on what you are saying.

An annoying habit adopted unconsciously by many speakers is that of swaying to and fro, either backward and forward or from side to side. This practice can induce a mild feeling of seasickness in your listeners and should be avoided at all costs. It also causes problems if you have a microphone, because your voice will be lurching in and out of earshot, rendering your speech a disaster.

Some speakers hop from one foot to the other and begin to form such an intricate pattern on the floor with their feet that they would rather look down to see what their feet are doing than at the audience. Listeners will strain to hear such speakers for a while, and then simply give up and wait for them to sit down.

Barriers

In our everyday life, we all put up barriers to hide behind, for our own safety. The position of a public speaker is very exposed, and the temptation to hide even greater than normal. You should try to conquer your fear, because it does communicate itself to the audience.

When you stand up to speak, you may be behind a table or lectern. Though a piece of furniture offers a form of protection to the less confident speaker, it also acts as a barrier between him or her and the audience, and any barriers to communication are undesirable. Make contact with the audience as directly as you can, and if possible, stand to the side of the table or lectern, where all can see you. Always opt for intimacy rather than distance.

Even experienced public speakers make small

gestures of self-protection as they stand to address an audience. These involve covering the body with one arm, maybe to fiddle with a cufflink or bracelet or to adjust an article of clothing. The less confident the speaker, the less well-disguised the gesture. You may find yourself raising your hand to touch the opposite side of your head, to smooth your hair, or scratch your ear. Try to avoid hugging yourself, crossing your arms, clasping one arm with the opposite hand, or rubbing your hands together, since these gestures obviously convey your nervousness.

An expressive voice

You should be able to put a lot of feeling into your voice, very much in the way an actor does, to make your speech come alive. If you are not used to public speaking, this will need practice. Someone with a good voice can make the most boring speech seem fascinating, but someone who speaks in a whining monotone can ruin anything, even Shakespeare.

Always speak in your natural voice. A surprising number of people assume a "stage" voice for speech-making, and this sounds as artificial as a specially cultivated telephone manner. Accents add distinctive character to any voice and should not be camouflaged.

Projection

Remember that unless you are provided with a microphone, your voice will have to carry to reach those at the very back of the hall. If you speak too softly, you will see your audience straining forward to hear you; after a while, some of them will give up in exasperation.

The key to voice projection is good breathing. If you

breathe shallowly, you will only be able to manage a few quiet words before you need to breathe again. Practice breathing deeply and speaking in a low, resonant voice from the bottom of your lungs. There is a difference between voice projection and shouting. Shouting at your audience is aggressive and will not endear you to them.

Pronunciation

As long as your audience can understand you, differences in pronunciation are completely acceptable. However, when it comes to proper names, you should always make sure you say them correctly or you risk causing offense. Check up on difficult names beforehand.

Clarity

Make sure you enunciate each word properly – i.e., pronounce each syllable clearly. This skill has nothing to do with regional accents. It involves mobility of the mouth and can be practiced in front of the mirror. The best way to practice is to exaggerate, pursing your lips, stretching them, using your tongue, your teeth, and the muscles of your throat.

Avoid running words together, like "dunno" for "don't know," and make sure you pronounce similar consonants precisely so that your audience can distinguish between "b," "d," and "t," for example. The less work the audience has to do to follow what you are saying, the easier you will find it to put your speech across.

Timing

Timing – where to insert pauses and when to let the words flow – is crucial if you want to give your speech drama and life. Good breathing will allow you to control the length of time you speak between pauses. If you breathe only shallowly, you will have to pause at regular, short intervals to draw breath, and this will destroy the shape of your sentences.

Pause in the natural places, as you would in conversation. You can allow a split-second pause for a comma; slightly longer for a semi-colon; and longer still for a period. Pause, too, within a sentence to give particular emphasis to dramatic words, as in "Never have so many/ owed so much/ to so few."

A pause of four or five seconds should announce the end of a paragraph, and don't be afraid of even longer pauses if you want to create suspense. Naturally, you should also pause to allow for laughter.

Strange though it may seem, mastery of silence is a powerful weapon in the armory of the public speaker. Make your silences active rather than passive by looking around searchingly at the faces of your audience, and they will respond with eager anticipation for your next words.

Emphasis

If you speak with quiet authority, you should be able to stress certain points without raising your voice in anger. Speakers who lose their temper lose control of their material, and will soon lose the respect of the listeners. It is often easier to shock, if that is your intention, by speaking the relevant phrase precisely and coolly than by exploding it into the air.

Try to put a natural roll into your phrases by varying your emphasis. Let your voice die down at the end of a sentence and rise to make a new point. A voice full of lively expression is much easier to listen to than a colorless monotone, for it communicates the fact that you yourself are interested in what you are saying.

75

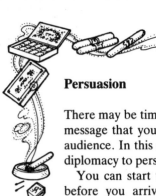

Persuasion

There may be times when you are called on to deliver a message that you know will not be welcomed by your audience. In this case, you need to use special tact and diplomacy to persuade them of the value of your views.

You can start to smooth the way for yourself even before you arrive at the meeting, by checking the schedule for the evening. If there will be several speakers and your speech is a tricky one, ask to speak first. If for some reason this is not possible, ask the chairman to ensure that the speakers preceding you do not go on too long, since your speech will certainly not succeed if it has to be cut short.

It is quite common for the chairman to agree to alert speakers who go over their time by passing them a card asking them to draw swiftly to a close. Of course, courtesy demands that speakers know in advance that this will happen to them if they continue for too long, and once they have been warned, the problem rarely occurs.

Breaking the ice

If your audience knows that you bring an unwelcome message, they may be predisposed not to like you, telling themselves that their minds are made up and that nothing you are about to say will alter the way they feel. On the other hand, they may be no more than suspicious of your efforts to begin with, but have their minds closed by the way you approach them. There are ways of breaking the ice and making sure that they gradually warm to you, or at least listen less than grudgingly instead of hardening their minds against you as you speak.

Begin with humor. Have a joke ready that shows that you appreciate their wariness of you. Making yourself the butt of your own joke is a very good way of thawing out your audience.

In your introductory remarks, make it clear that you admire their achievements. Praise them in some detail to show that you have done your research into their organization. Don't be obsequious or fawning, because this won't convince anybody, but if you are genuine in your admiration and understanding of their aims, you will establish a common ground between yourself and the audience. They will then be more inclined to think of you as a reasonable person whose opinions are worth listening to.

Your tone of voice

Your tone of voice is crucial, especially as you get into the body of a speech that will present the audience with some unpalatable truths.

* Remain good-humored at all times. Remember, your job is to get the audience on your side, and you are not likely to succeed in this aim if you rush in and bash them over the head with a hammer or leap up and stick your fangs into their jugular. You may release your own frustrations, but you will surely transfer your irritation and anger to your listeners.

* Don't let your voice become aggressive, no matter how passionately you feel about the subject; instead, use gentle reasoning to persuade them of the worth of your argument. Be wary of falling into the opposite trap, that of assuming yourself to be in a superior position and condescending to correct them. A self-opinionated speaker will earn only contempt for his cause.

* Avoid arguing, pushing, and picking on your audience; they will only recoil. Instead, be polite, friendly, relaxed.

How to win them over
No one is ever more convinced of anything than when they think it was their own idea in the first place. If you let the audience come to their own conclusion in agreement with yours, your victory will be the greater, because their defeat is painless. A skillful speaker will have the pleasure of seeing the audience warm so much to the message that they adopt it as their own without any loss of face.

* Never attack your audience directly. Instead, use parallel examples, vividly illustrated, and let them make the connections themselves to their own attitudes or behavior.

78

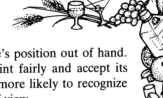

* Never dismiss your audience's position out of hand. Always consider their viewpoint fairly and accept its worth; that way, they will be more likely to recognize the worth of your own point of view.

* If you think they are wrong, don't give them the impression that you think they are all idiots. Instead, show them you feel they are reasonable people who have, in this instance, been misguided. Show your concern by telling them why you think their misguided idea will backfire, damaging the good reputation of their organization.

* If you can see a way to shift the blame from your listeners, do so. Perhaps you can blame what you see as the error of their ways on misinformation, for example. In this case, you can assure them they have done the best they could with the information available while convincing them that they haven't been given the full picture.

* It's always a winning move to be able to present your case with new evidence that your audience has not heard up to now. This makes it quite easy for them to change sides without losing face.

* Build the evidence for your case piece by piece and subtly. Quote sources and support for the information you present. Overwhelm them – but gradually – with the sheer force and weight of your argument.

* Point out to them what will happen if they follow their present policy. Show convincingly that it will lead to disaster. Do this with consideration and without crowing over the picture you paint. Make it clear that they can save themselves from embarrassment.

THE SECRETS OF GOOD LISTENING

One of the things that helps a public speaker succeed, and that makes his or her speech memorable, is the quality of the audience. Every one of us has sat quietly at some time and listened to someone else making a speech, whether at a business meeting, a school reunion, or a wedding anniversary party. But many people occupy their seats without having any idea of how to listen, and even the most experienced speaker can fail miserably when he rejoins the audience and takes his turn at paying attention to someone else.

If you want to give a speaker all the consideration you would want for yourself, the most important thing to do is to look at him. Eye contact expresses your interest immediately, and common courtesy demands it. No one likes to talk to a blank wall or a roomful of listeners gazing into their laps, so be sure your eyes establish for the speaker that your ears are open and ready.

Let the speaker know how closely you are following his points by nodding, smiling, or laughing aloud at his jokes. The gestures and body language are exactly the same as those you would use in ordinary conversation, and they're equally appropriate in more formal circumstances.

Let your face speak for you. Standing behind the podium or lectern, the speaker will not be able to tell if he has somehow confused or misled you unless he can read it in your expression. Interruptions are not common during formally prepared speeches, but your face can be as elequent as a voice and your expression will carry from the very back of the room.

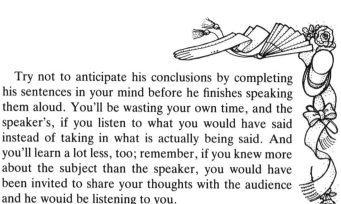

Try not to anticipate his conclusions by completing his sentences in your mind before he finishes speaking them aloud. You'll be wasting your own time, and the speaker's, if you listen to what you would have said instead of taking in what is actually being said. And you'll learn a lot less, too; remember, if you knew more about the subject than the speaker, you would have been invited to share your thoughts with the audience and he wouid be listening to you.

Concentrate on what you're hearing. Letting the sound of the speaker's voice fill your ears while your thoughts are full of tomorrow's appointments or Saturday's picnic robs you of an opportunity to participate. It shortchanges the speaker, too, because it robs him of the very audience he is working so hard to entertain or educate.

You may have the chance to ask questions at the completion of the prepared remarks. In that case, you will be able to clarify any points that have confused you, obtain a little additional information in some area of the subject that particularly interests you, and possibly open the topic to further discussion, by either the speaker or the other members of the audience. They will be grateful for your contribution, and you will have the satisfaction of knowing you are an active and useful listener instead of a bump on a log.

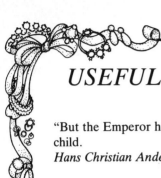

USEFUL QUOTATIONS

"But the Emperor has nothing on at all!", cried a little child.
Hans Christian Andersen

The nearer the Church, the farther from God.
Bishop Lancelot Andrews

After coitus every animal is sad.
Anonymous

Law is a bottomless pit.
Dr. Arbuthnot

One small step for man, one giant leap for mankind.
Neil Armstrong

Oh I see said the Earl but my own idear is that these things are as piffle before the wind.
Daisy Ashford

A shilling life will give you all the facts.
W.H. Auden

Blessed is the person who is too busy to worry in the daytime, and too sleepy to worry at night.
Leo Aikman

The more alternatives, the more difficult the choice.
Abbé d'Allainval

More will mean worse.
Kingsley Amis

Goodness is easier to recognize than to define.
W.H. Auden

An egg boiled very soft is not unwholesome.
Jane Austen, Emma

Silence is the virtue of fools.
Francis Bacon

The worst solitude is to be destitute of sincere friendship.
Francis Bacon

The second blow makes the fray.
Francis Bacon

As long as I have want, I have reason for living. Satisfaction is death.
George Bernard Shaw

He that wrestles with us strengthens our nerves and sharpens our skill. Our antagonist is our helper.
Edmund Burke

People will not look forward to posterity who never look backward to their ancestors.
Edmund Burke

An after-dinner speech should be like a lady's dress – long enough to cover the subject and short enough to be interesting.
R.A. Butler

A committee is an animal with four back legs.
John Le Carré

The world will never starve for want of wonders; but only for want of wonder.
G.K. Chesterton

Men occasionally stumble over the truth, but most of them pick themselves up and hurry off as if nothing had happened.
Winston Churchill

Give us the tools, and we will finish the job.
Winston Churchill

This is not the end. It is not even the beginning of the end. But it is, perhaps, the end of the beginning.
Winston Churchill

There is no finer investment for any community than putting milk into babies.
Winston Churchill

A fanatic is one who can't change his mind and won't change the subject.
Winston Churchill

Times change, and we change with them.
Classical

There is nothing ugly; I never saw an ugly thing in my life: for let the form of an object be what it may – light, shade, and perspective will always make it beautiful.
John Constable

When there is no peril in the fight, there is no glory in the triumph.
Corneille

No man is a hero to his valet.
Mme. Cornuel

The youth of a nation are the trustees of posterity.
Benjamin Disraeli

We cannot eat the fruit while the tree is in blossom.
Benjamin Disraeli

Can anybody remember when times were not hard and money not scarce?
Ralph Waldo Emerson

They can conquer who believe they can.
Ralph Waldo Emerson

A little neglect may breed mischief; for want of a nail the shoe was lost; for want of a shoe the horse was lost; for want of a horse the rider was lost.
Benjamin Franklin

There is a sufficiency in the world for man's need but not for man's greed.
Mahatma Gandhi

The true use of speech is not so much to express our wants as to conceal them.
Oliver Goldsmith

Doctors are lucky. The sun sees their successes; the earth covers their mistakes.
Greek saying

Go West, young man, and grow up with the country.
Horace Greeley

But did thee feel the earth move?
Ernest Hemingway

Envy is an admission of inferiority.
Victor Hugo

Danger for danger's sake is senseless.
Leigh Hunt

You ain't heard nothin' yet, folks.
Al Jolson

The Vicar of St. Ives says the smell of fish there is
sometimes so terrific as to stop the church clock.
Rev. Francis Kilvert

Error of opinion may be tolerated where reason is left
free to combat it.
Thomas Jefferson

A journey of a thousand miles begins with a single step.
Lao-Tze

You can fool some of the people all the time and all of
the people some of the time, but you can't fool all of
the people all of the time.
Abraham Lincoln (attributed)

The ballot is stronger than the bullet.
Abraham Lincoln

There's no getting blood out of a turnip.
Captain Marryat

Morality is the herd instinct in the individual.
Friedrich Nietzsche

Believe me! The secret of reaping the greatest fruitfulness and the greatest enjoyment from life is to live dangerously!
Friedrich Nietzsche

You can't teach an old dogma new tricks.
Dorothy Parker

Had Cleopatra's nose been shorter, the whole history of the world would have changed.
Blaise Pascal

We shall die alone.
Blaise Pascal

Where observation is concerned, chance favors only the prepared mind.
Louis Pasteur

Blessed is he who expects nothing, for he shall never be disappointed.
Alexander Pope

Don't go into Mr. McGregor's garden: your Father had an accident there; he was put in a pie by Mrs. McGregor.
Beatrix Potter

Wisdom is knowledge tempered with judgement.
Lord Ritchie-Calder

Everyone complains of his memory, but no one complains of his judgment.
François, Duc de la Rochefoucauld

Don't let yesterday take up too much of today.
Will Rogers

Everything is funny as long as it's happening to somebody else.
Will Rogers

Being a hero is about the shortest-lived profession on earth.
Will Rogers

I don't make jokes – I just watch the government and report the facts.
Will Rogers

Get someone else to blow your trumpet and the sound will carry twice as far.
Will Rogers

I used to tell my husband that, if he could make *me* understand something, it would be clear to all the other people in the country.
Eleanor Roosevelt

A radical is a man with both feet planted firmly in the air.
Franklin Delano Roosevelt

No man is justified in doing evil on the ground of expediency.
Theodore Roosevelt

For an idea ever to be fashionable is ominous, since it must afterwards be old-fashioned.
George Santayana

Small is beautiful.
Professor E.F. Schumacher

Great God! this is an awful place.
Captain Scott, of the South Pole

Nobody heard him, the dead man,
But still he lay moaning:
I was much further out than you thought
And not waving but drowning.
Stevie Smith

No matter how thin you slice it, it's still baloney.
A.E. Smith

We can all be angry with our neighbor. What we want is to be shown, not his defects of which we are too conscious, but his merits to which we are too blind.
R.L. Stevenson

You can fool too many of the people too much of the time.
James Thurber

If you want to be happy, be.
Leo Tolstoy

There were times when my pants were so thin I could sit on a dime and tell if it was heads or tails.
Spencer Tracy

He is a fool who thinks by force or skill
To turn the current of a woman's will.
Samuel Tooke (1673)

There are three kinds of lies: lies, damned lies, and statistics.
Mark Twain

Reports of my death are greatly exaggerated.
Mark Twain

Man is the only animal that blushes. Or needs to.
Mark Twain

I have a prodigious quantity of mind; it takes me as much as a week, sometimes, to make it up.
Mark Twain

The radical invents the views. When he has worn them out, the conservative adopts them.
Mark Twain

This is petrified truth.
Mark Twain

He is now fast rising from affluence to poverty.
Mark Twain

An experienced, industrious, ambitious, and often quite picturesque liar.
Mark Twain

Familiarity breeds contempt – and children.
Mark Twain

Since wars begin in the minds of men, it is in the minds of men that the defenses of peace must be constructed.
Constitution of UNESCO

A healthy male adult bore consumes each year one and a half times his own weight in other people's patience.
John Updike

In making up a party for a traveling excursion, always be sure to include one ignorant person who will ask all the questions you are ashamed to ask, and you will acquire a great deal of information you would otherwise lose.
Charles Dudley Warner

Labor to keep alive in your breast that little spark of celestial fire – conscience.
George Washington

There is no sin except stupidity.
Oscar Wilde

The truth is rarely pure, and never simple.
Oscar Wilde

There is only one thing in the world worse than being talked about, and that is not being talked about.
Oscar Wilde

We are all in the gutter, but some of us are looking at the stars.
Oscar Wilde

As long as war is regarded as wicked, it will always have its fascination. When it is looked upon as vulgar, it will cease to be popular.
Oscar Wilde

Work is the curse of the drinking classes.
Oscar Wilde

It is only about things that do not interest one that one can give a really unbiased opinion, which is no doubt the reason why an unbiased opinion is always valueless.
Oscar Wilde

I shall not say why and how I became, at the age of fifteen, the mistress of the Earl of Craven.
Harriette Wilson, Memoirs, *first sentence*

The only time losing is more fun than winning is when you're fighting temptation.
Tom Wilson

A knife of the keenest steel requires the whetstone, and the wisest man needs advice.
Zoroaster

INDEX